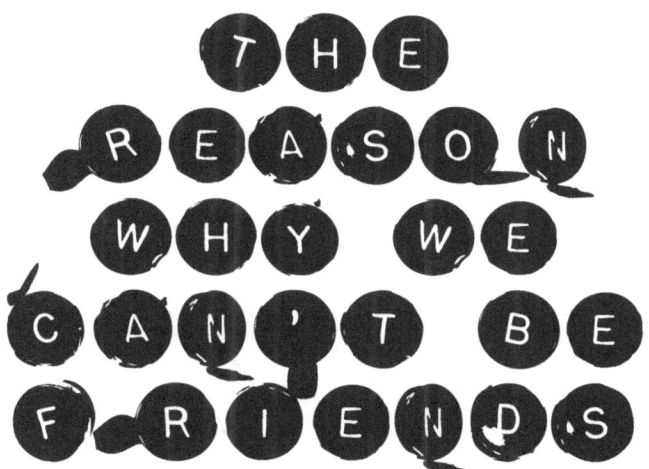

by
Mark Nicholls

This first edition published in Australia in 2019 by:

Prahran Publishing
P.O. Box 2041, Prahran, Victoria, 3181

© Copyright Mark Nicholls 2019

Mark Nicholls has asserted his legal and moral right under the Copyright Act 1968 to be identified as the author of this work.

Published by arrangement with
Prahran Publishing, Australia.

All rights are strictly reserved.

No part of this publication may be reproduced, stored in a retrieval system or transmitted, in any form or by any other means, without the publisher's prior permission in writing. Copying of this script for performance reasons is also strictly prohibited by law, either in whole or excerpts from.

This book is sold subject to the condition that it shall not, by way of trade or otherwise, be lent, resold, hired out or otherwise circulated without the publisher's prior consent in any form of binding or cover other than that in which it is published and without similar condition, including this condition, being imposed on the subsequent purchaser.

Every reasonable effort has been made to trace copyright holders of material reproduced in this book, but if any have been inadvertently overlooked the publishers would be glad to hear from them. The story, all names, characters, and incidents portrayed in this book are fictitious. No identification with actual persons past or present, places, buildings, and products is intended or should be inferred.

ISBN 978-1-922263-02-5 Paperback
ISBN 978-1-922263-03-2 eBook

Dewey: 822.4

A catalogue record for this
book is available from the
National Library of Australia

Performance Licensing and Royalty Payments

Mark Nicholls retains control of both the amateur and professional stage performance rights of this play. No unauthorised performance should occur without the express and written permission of the playwright.

Restriction of Alteration

There shall be no modifications of any kind to the play including deletion of dialogue (including objectionable language), changes to characters gender or names, title of the play or music without the express and written permission from the author.

Sound and Video Recordings

This play may contain stage directions to include the use of music, video or other sound recordings either in part or in whole. The author and the publisher have not sought the right to use such content and performance rights permission should be obtained seperately. Permission to record audio and video recordings of all performances must also be explicitly given by the author in writing.

Author Credit

Performance rights approval requires credit be given to Mark Nicholls as the sole and exclusive author of the play. This obligation applies to the title page of every program or other advertising material distributed in connection to this play. The author's credit should appear immediately under the title of the play on all published material, and alongside no other individual. Font size of credit cannot be less than 50% of the largest letter used in the play's title.

Please email info@prahran.press
for all performance enquiries.

*In memory of Cassandra Jean Laing
1968-2007,*

painter, friend, unconventional woman.

About the Playwright

MARK NICHOLLS has been performing on various Melbourne stages since the age of six and has an extensive list of credits as a playwright, composer, singer, actor, producer and director. He is Senior Lecturer in Cinema Studies at the University of Melbourne where he has taught film since 1993.

He is the author of *Lost Objects of Desire: The Performances of Jeremy Irons* (2012), *Scorsese's Men: Melancholia and the Mob* (2004) and recently published articles on Italian Cinema, Powell and Pressburger's *The Red Shoes* and Sergei Diaghilev's celebrated company, The Ballets Russes.

Mark is a film critic and worked for many years on ABC Radio and for *The Age* newspaper, for which he wrote a weekly column between 2007 and 2009.

He lives in Melbourne with his partner, Ali Wirtz, and their two sons Oscar and Carlo.

SERIES PREFACE

I wrote these plays for only one reason, to perform them. I publish them here, therefore, somewhat reluctantly. They were never written to be read on the page by anyone but a treasured posy of performers that I trust to help me rescue them from it. They were certainly never conceived of as works of anything so respectable as literature. Nevertheless, I have found two reasons to overcome my reluctance and my usual roguish prejudice against readers and writers in favour of performers and punters. One reason is that putting these plays into print provides the opportunity for the most engaged of those who saw and heard them to revive and revise the experience. The other reason is archival. I wish to leave a permanent, if inadequate, record of the facts of their production over a decade, in a private space in Melbourne, for the benefit of both a small, dedicated paying audience, and for a smaller band of compulsive show-folk.

Writing these plays for the talented actors, musicians and backstage characters whose creations are recorded here, and having the privilege of working with these artists to produce them, has been the most satisfying occupation of my otherwise horrendously charmed and fascinating life.

Now that they have had their blessed release in print, these plays are beyond the concern of any motivation I had to write them. Read them, o curious one, and work it out for yourself! One motivation I will record, however, rests in the inspiration generously given by those who worked on and attended these cosy performances, and so brought their privileged, fleeting moments of theatre securely into being.

ABOUT THE PLAY

I began to write this play, under the Almodóvarian title, *Outing My Mother*, some years earlier than it was finally staged. I quickly found that this farce was going nowhere, especially as it became clear to me that I had written "the mother", as my own mother would certainly have referred to her, in such a way that it could only have been played by Barry Humphries frocking-up as Dame Edna Everage. Mr Humphries and I share a high school tie, a common tertiary alma mater and undergraduate major, but I doubt these questionable bonds would have obligated him to take on the role, even if he knew I grew up in Moonee Ponds.

Despite the fact that it had an earlier genesis, this play entered life as a sequel to *Somewhere Between Three Rehearsals and the Performance*, which was about the same characters, set ten years earlier and performed two years before in 2008. Some part of the mammadrama that was, still remains in this play. It merges with a sort of therapy comedy that I had originally envisaged, but this version is liberally peppered with the sort of showfolk business, which always seems to me to be the only real sign of life. Hence the song, 'The thing I like best is getting ready', the sentiment of which I endorse so wholeheartedly that I expect to hear some kind friend sing it at my funeral.

Singing the 'Mrs Worthington Blues', Grace Taylor played one of the most beautiful bits of theatre I never saw – I was too busy panicking at the piano and had my back to her – but I could hear every word of the world-weary exhaustion she brilliantly conjured as Imogen, the dutiful theatre daughter, born in a trunk, burning with energy, destined to a life lived without dignity and pickled in gin. 'Take, oh take my soul for it's eternal' is the sort of interior and heartfelt business that Madeleine Swain can manage before breakfast – and, of course, she did. I am particularly proud of this little song because I wrote it in the shower and it fulfilled my ambition to write a melancholy lament in the very unmelancholy key of C major.

Considering my mother, Barry Humphries and Dame Edna, it now seems obvious that only Caerwen Martin could have done such manic justice to Ellen, the mother of the final version. In doing so, another page of drag-queen stage maternity history was left mercifully unturned. I welcome this and consider it just. I suspect most writers are faithless to their muses, and their mothers, in the end.

CHARACTERS

ELLEN: forty-two, an actor, manic promoter and sometimes mother.

LANA: forty-four, a psychoanalyst.

GLENN: forty-six, an actor and nowadays less manic promoter.

IMOGEN: nineteen, a born actor in search of her own career.

The play is set here and now in spring.

The Reason Why We Can't Be Friends was first performed at Rear 4, Clifton Hill Victoria on the 17th of March 2011 with the following cast:

Ellen:	Caerwen Martin
Lana:	Madeleine Swain
Glenn:	Mark Nicholls
Imogen:	Grace Taylor
Director:	Mark Nicholls
Associate Director:	Anika Ervin-Ward
Co Producer:	Alison Wirtz

PROLOGUE

> *IMOGEN is on stage in the middle of a performance of a well-known comic song inspired by the great Noel Coward but set to a melancholic tune and lyrics by the present, far from great, songster. IMOGEN is sitting at a dressing table and mournfully singing as she removes her stage make-up.*

IMOGEN: [sings]
Don't put your daughter on the stage,
Mrs Worthington,
Don't put your daughter on the stage.
There'll be lessons in elocution,
How to dance and how to sing,
But before you know it,
She'll be off with some poet
And talking all left wing.

Kids have got no toys to play with
Papa's got no booze,
Mrs Worthington's got no time
to sing the blues.

Don't put your daughter on the stage,
Mrs Worthington,
Don't put your daughter on the stage.
There'll be tears and histrionics,
With every half-baked play,
She'll do drugs, she'll do late night parties,
She'll probably end up gay.

Kids have got no private school fees
Papa's got no shoes,
Mrs Worthington's got no right
to sing the blues.

I'm telling ya fellas,
Mrs Worthington's got no right
to sing the blues.

Fade lights. End scene.

In a theatre foyer following the show GLENN and ELLEN are standing aside while the audience are indulging in the ritual of the opening night party. They are removed from the proceedings despite the fact that it is their party. ELLEN is power-dressed and regards the scene as a thing of business. GLENN is obviously not long offstage and, while sharing ELLEN's concerns, still hopes someone will come up and tell him how marvellous he was. He has softened a little in ten years, become less ambitious and busy. ELLEN has gone the other way. She is in no way the under-confident would-be stage success she was ten years ago.

ELLEN: Everyone knows that lighting designer is a disaster. I should never have used him. No wonder the pre-sales are down.

GLENN: The design is fine. Don't worry about it.

ELLEN: Emma didn't show up. Neither did Daniel.

GLENN: It's amazing how you can manage to fill the house and you are still concerned about a few theatre types who didn't show up.

ELLEN: Yeah, well, they are actors, they are supposed to show up.

GLENN: No they're not. It's only the real punters that count.

ELLEN: Yes but isn't it funny how it's the theatre people who never seem to show... They are probably annoyed that we never cast them.

GLENN: It's more likely they are annoyed there's no Equity concession.

ELLEN: I'm not going to start comp-ing actors and directors just so that they can bitch about me for free. If people want to bitch about me they can pay for it. The point is they don't like it when I cast Imogen. Emma still fantasises that she can play a nineteen-year-old.

GLENN: So did you until relatively recently.

ELLEN: But they may have a point about Imogen. She was far too flat tonight.

GLENN: It's opening night. No one here expects it to be really ready for at least three weeks.

ELLEN: Yeah, well, she'll be pushing it to make three weeks. That's if we actually manage to run that long.

GLENN: I suppose she is a bit dry in this one.

ELLEN: Dry? The girl's incapable of tearing up over anything. They don't want stoic suffering they want uncontrollable blubbering.

Act I - Scene I

GLENN: [Looking off across the room] Yeah, it's really quite sick how audiences want to pay for youth and beauty and then they want to watch her pay for it.

LANA enters from stage left. Only ELLEN sees her.

ELLEN: [To herself] My God. That's Lana!

LANA: Hello Ellen!

ELLEN: I suppose it would be stupid to say long time no see?

GLENN still has not noticed her.

LANA: I don't see why.

ELLEN: Glenn, you remember Lana!

GLENN has not engaged at all.

GLENN: Yes. Excuse me a minute, there's some untapped sponsorship just over there. I'll be back in a minute.

GLENN rushes off.

ELLEN: He hasn't changed in ten years!

LANA: No.

They laugh.

ELLEN: I can't believe you're here. It's been such a long time.

LANA: Actually, I'm here in a professional capacity. You rang our counselling service to make an appointment.

ELLEN: What? Hang on. You mean, you're working for the shrink service I called last week?

LANA: Carlton Health. Yes.

ELLEN: And they sent you to speak to me?

LANA: They made an appointment for us to meet.

ELLEN: How bizarre! I mean, it's just such a coincidence.

LANA: Not really. You'd be amazed who calls.

ELLEN: Well I don't want to cause you any embarrassment. Perhaps I should call the office and arrange to see someone else?

LANA: Are you embarrassed?

ELLEN: To be honest, I am still shocked at actually seeing you here. But wouldn't it be slightly unorthodox for me to see you?

LANA: Only if you are uncomfortable about it. It is probably no more unorthodox than me turning up here to see you at work.

ELLEN: Do you mean that you came here specifically to start our sessions?

LANA: We can talk now if you like.

ELLEN: And that you knew it was me when they gave you the case?

LANA: Who else could it have been? You are fairly exposed – especially lately. Of course if you don't consider it professionally appropriate for me to see you, I can always suggest someone else.

ELLEN: No, I didn't mean that. It's just such a shock.

LANA: Are you OK?

GLENN is waving ELLEN over.

ELLEN: No. I mean, yes. That's not what I meant. Look, I probably should mingle and we can't talk here, anyway. Are you around this weekend? I've got a lot to talk to you about.

LANA: That's what I'm here for.

GLENN: [Calling] Ellen, come and meet Dame Mary.

ELLEN: Fine. [To LANA] Look, how about we meet...

LANA: Don't worry, I'll find you.

GLENN: [Calling] Ellen!

ELLEN: What?

LANA: [Leaving] Bye Ellen.

ELLEN: OK. [To GLENN] For God's sake Glenn.

GLENN: Sorry I just wanted you to chat up Dame Mary.

ELLEN: Well, where is she?

GLENN: She's gone off after that young waiter with a glass of champagne.

ELLEN: But he's serving the food!

GLENN: No, no, no she's taking the champagne to him! Anyway, who was that?

ELLEN: My psychologist apparently.

GLENN: And you know her?

ELLEN: Glenn, you idiot, that was Lana!

GLENN: Lana, Lana?

ELLEN: Lana.

GLENN: My Lana? God, I didn't recognise her at all.

ELLEN: You were too worried about Dame Mary and that cute waiter.

GLENN: She's a psychologist? I thought she went into that psych ward as a patient?

ELLEN: So did I.

GLENN: So the fruitcake is now a shrink and she's gonna try to sort you out?

Act I - Scene I

ELLEN: She's not a fruitcake.

GLENN: You said she was.

ELLEN: That was ten years ago. And I never really found out what happened there anyway.

GLENN: Yeah, well you're the fruitcake if you see her. Talk about the idiots running the asylum.

IMOGEN enters and looks about.

ELLEN: Imogen. Finally.

IMOGEN walks straight to LANA and they embrace.

GLENN: And I think it's all about to get a little nuttier.

LANA: [To IMOGEN] Hello darling!

IMOGEN: Lana! I'm so glad you're here.

ELLEN: My God!

Lights fade. End scene.

SCENE TWO

The theatre foyer as before, but now set up for a rehearsal. GLENN and ELLEN are rehearsing.

GLENN: [Sings]:
It's just a dream I have, waiting to come true
It's just a dream I have, these crazy thoughts of you
I try to think of other girls,
but no one else will do
It's just a dream I have and that dream is you.

It's just a dream I have, a coffee klatch for two,
It's just a dream I have, long black with sugar too
I tried drinking an espresso
but a quick one just won't do
It's just a dream I have, a coffee klatch for two.

It's just a dream I have, a luncheon meet with you
It's just a dream I have, three courses and wine too
I tried sushi from a bento box,
but cold fish will never do
It's just a dream I have, a luncheon meet with you.

It's just a dream I have, a supper rendezvous
It's just a dream I have, a private room chez nous
I tried sipping bedtime cocoa,
but the sweetness all fell through
It's just a dream I have, a supper rendezvous.

It's just a dream I have, waiting to come true
It's just a dream I have, one square meal with you.
I've tried many a fine dining option,
but none of them came through
Because the dream I have is just a dream of you.

ELLEN: All that food makes me feel sick. But it'll do I suppose. Where the hell is Imogen? *[She shuffles some music. She is manic.]* What do you think is going on between those two?

GLENN: I have no idea. She never mentioned Lana to me.

ELLEN: Are you sure?

GLENN: I think I would have remembered.

ELLEN: Surely Lana wouldn't stalk Imogen to get back at me?

GLENN: I doubt it.

ELLEN: Well you know what they're like.

GLENN: They?

ELLEN: Don't pretend to be stupid. You know exactly what I mean.

GLENN: Do I?

ELLEN: Do you think Imogen's gay?

GLENN: What?

ELLEN: Do you think she knows about me and Lana? Perhaps she's just cooked the whole thing up to get back at me. She always blamed me for the divorce. She always took Malcolm's side.

GLENN: That's totally unfair. Not to mention illogical.

ELLEN: Well, something really weird is going on here. Imogen's been sulky and difficult all through rehearsals. Last night she walked through the entire show like she was asleep and then she parades Lana in the damn foyer right in front of my face. She's obviously trying to get at me.

GLENN: Ellen stop it.

ELLEN: What do you mean?

GLENN: Just stop. You're going nuts.

ELLEN: Don't be absurd.

GLENN: You're being absurd. You're totally losing it. *[Interrupting her]* Just stop!

ELLEN: *[Takes a breath]* What?

GLENN: It's a coincidence. Imi obviously has no idea that you know Lana. She certainly has no reason to bring her here to rub your face in it – so to speak. You have got to calm down. You are going crazy. You would be better to concentrate on helping her. She's flat. She tries really hard but she's not a natural. She has to work harder than you do and she needs direction.

ELLEN: I'm not running a school for actors. She's not some kid we plucked off the street. God she had an agent and an Equity card before any of us did.

GLENN: It's easier for cute kid actors.

ELLEN: Well, it's not as if she doesn't know how to do it. She has been on the job since she was eight. She's just being slack.

GLENN: Yeah. She had a normal childhood before that.

ELLEN: You mean dull.

GLENN: Well at least it was her own.

ELLEN: No it wasn't, it was Malcolm's. Dull. What's the point? Imogen and I are stuck together in this thing, this business, and we just don't get on.

GLENN: Perhaps it's a good thing Lana turned up. We could get her in for some family therapy sessions. We could wheel in Malcolm too.

ELLEN: *[Laughs and finally relaxes]* You can forget about that.

GLENN: Why, she's a professional psychologist.

ELLEN: Last night you were calling her a fruitcake.

GLENN: Whatever happened there anyway? I never really heard the full story.

ELLEN: I don't really know what happened, to be honest. After your blasted play we kept seeing each other for about six months. We were very close. And then we weren't. She wouldn't take my phone calls. She didn't return my emails. It became one of those text message relationships. After a while that was the only

Act 1 - Scene 2

way we could communicate. I tried to find out why, but she wouldn't tell me. She just cut me off and that's it. That was ten years ago and I think I've thought about her once a week ever since.

GLENN: Did you screw her?

ELLEN: Glenn straight to the point as usual. No, I didn't 'screw' her in, any way.

GLENN: Did you want to?

ELLEN: No. Maybe. Probably!

GLENN: So you wanted to sleep with her, she didn't want to sleep with you so she dumped you. What's the big deal? It's not an unfamiliar scenario, especially with you.

ELLEN: Thinking of anyone in particular, darling?

GLENN: Perhaps.

ELLEN: Well I did sleep with you, so it's not a very good comparison.

GLENN: But I did dump you.

ELLEN: I don't want to go there.

GLENN: OK. So you wanted her, you never got her, and ever since that you still want her. That is to say, you never got over her because you never got one. It's called nostalgia darling.

ELLEN: Perhaps, but it's not quite so sexually dependent as you like to think. It was one of those very intense relationships you have when you're young and stupid.

GLENN: What, full of long Victorian letters, packed with reading suggestions and plagiarism?

ELLEN: Something like that. God, you're cynical. I'd like to know what you were doing at the time.

GLENN: Well, I wasn't swanning round drinking mulled wine and misquoting Wordsworth.

ELLEN: Yes, it shows.

GLENN: Well this little encounter should provide the perfect opportunity to pick up where you left off and find out what the hell happened.

ELLEN: If I agree to see her.

GLENN: You know you will. But I have a word of warning for you if you do.

ELLEN: If you are going to get serious I don't want to hear it.

GLENN: No, I'm not being serious, I'm being considerate and truthful – you know the sort of things real people do for their friends, as opposed to what crazy fantasy dream chicks do.

ELLEN: Oh darling, how touching.

Act 1 - Scene 2

GLENN: If you are going to be sarcastic, I'm going to be blunt. It may just be that, although to your intensely romantic private school sentimentality, this brief encounter was highly significant, to her it might have been just one of those things. She's obviously nuts, and highly suspect, to go for this thing in the first place. I wouldn't put it past her to be devious as well.

ELLEN: Do you know I almost had the impression she didn't really know who I was.

GLENN: Now you're getting paranoid. Didn't you say that when she came over to you, she seemed to know you better than I do.

ELLEN: Except, of course, for the sex bit.

GLENN: Get over it.

ELLEN: I know. It's just that I got this funny feeling about the way she approached me. Given that we've both been living in Melbourne for the last ten years and I haven't seen her, you would think she must have avoided me at least five times before now. But last night she came bounding up to me, packed full of confidence, and totally unaffected by the whole thing.

GLENN: She's probably just changed and she feels slightly absurd about the past – which is why she's working so hard now. No one with her emotional CV is ever totally unaffected.

ELLEN: Or she has simply repressed the whole thing?

GLENN: Which is psycho-babble for, she's totally forgotten all about you.

ELLEN: You brought up the emotional CV idea.

GLENN: Yeah, I was talking about her but I was thinking about you.

ELLEN: What you think I'm neurotic?

GLENN: Well, how do I know you ever really knew her that well? I don't remember you spending much time together when we did the show. It may be all in your mind. I suspect that if I asked her about it there might be an embarrassing little stalker story there for my amusement.

ELLEN: So how do you account for her knowing more about me than you do? Apart from the sex bit.

GLENN: I expect she reads the arts pages. She could have easily put together a little bio on you in, say, half an hour?

ELLEN: Well, that makes her the stalker then.

GLENN: No, she's just doing her job.

ELLEN: She's hardly doing her job very professionally if she agrees to turn up here and be my analyst, given that she knows me.

GLENN: But that's just it. She doesn't know you!

Enter IMOGEN.

Act 1 - Scene 2

ELLEN: You're late.

IMOGEN: I know. I'm sorry. I went out with some uni friends after the show and we didn't get home 'til late.

ELLEN: You managed to remember that we have a show tonight.

IMOGEN: Obviously. That's why I am here.

ELLEN: Did you get any comments from anyone?

IMOGEN: Yeah.

ELLEN: What like?

IMOGEN: Everyone thought it was fine.

ELLEN: Anything more specific?

IMOGEN: I don't know. When do you ever care what the punters think?

ELLEN: I meant about your performance.

IMOGEN: Well, my friends are hardly going to tell me if they thought I sucked.

ELLEN: They can't be very good friends then.

IMOGEN: Like your legions of friends!

GLENN: If it's going to be one of those rehearsals, I'll leave it to you.

GLENN exits.

IMOGEN: So, what was so bad about it, anyway? Did I bump into the furniture?

ELLEN: That would have been a lively alternative to your performance.

IMOGEN: What?

ELLEN: It's all technical and gen Y attitude, there's no emotion.

IMOGEN: I'm going minimalist with it. If I let it all go we're going to get laughed off the stage.

ELLEN: Minimalist? It's a melodrama. I know that's all a bit lowbrow for you and your cutting edge uni friends but it's what real people want.

IMOGEN: A mother-daughter melodrama, is it? I don't think we would really be believable in that, do you 'Mum'?

ELLEN: It's not about being believable. We're not supposed to be doing the feeling, they are. That's why they come.

IMOGEN: Well, if that is the way you want it, you should do it. Stand up in the middle of the stage and wear your heart on your sleeve for ninety minutes. You'll have just the same effect. I'll sit in the corner and play the cello to pump up their heartstrings a bit.

Act I - Scene 2

ELLEN: It's not the music that does it, it's the ingénue. Nasty mothers and suffering, innocent daughters. Or the other way around! Anyway, that means you.

IMOGEN: Any other notes?

ELLEN: Just try to look like you are enjoying it.

IMOGEN exits. Ellen starts working at a table and drinking coffee. LANA enters and sits.

ELLEN: I thought you'd abandoned me.

LANA: You've been so busy. Besides, I only really came to observe.

ELLEN: So, we don't start the sessions until we get into your office?

LANA: It doesn't have to be as structured as all that. We can talk now if you need to.

ELLEN: Where do we start?

LANA: I would have thought you might want to begin with your daughter.

ELLEN: She has been the big drawcard this weekend, hasn't she?

LANA: How do you feel about that?

ELLEN: Why should I feel anything at all?

LANA: It wouldn't be the first time a mother has felt uneasy about her daughter getting all the attention.

ELLEN: Which is why I'm not uneasy about it.

LANA: It doesn't depress you?

ELLEN: Depress me? No. In fact, I couldn't have written it better. It is exactly the kind of thing my plays are supposed to be about.

LANA: Is that why you keep doing them?

ELLEN: Not exactly.

LANA: Is there any reason you chose this week to ring for counselling?

ELLEN: Once the new play is up and running I expect to have more time to indulge myself.

LANA: Indulge? What did you want to talk about?

ELLEN: You!

LANA: Yes?

ELLEN: Actually, I wanted to talk about you.

LANA: Why did you want to talk about me?

ELLEN: I suppose I wanted to know why you abandoned me.

LANA: Why do you think that I abandoned you?

Act I - Scene 2

ELLEN: Because when I needed you, you weren't there.

LANA: Why did you need me?

ELLEN: I am not really sure. Perhaps I just needed you to help with the lack of you.

LANA: What was so special about me?

ELLEN: I didn't know anyone like you. I admired you. I don't know. Do we ever really know what makes someone special to us?

LANA: What comes into your mind when you think about me?

ELLEN: The fact that you left.

LANA: What else?

ELLEN: Your little comforts.

LANA: What does that mean?

ELLEN: Don't you remember? You use to call them your 'little comforts'. Shakespeare, music and long afternoon walks, all designed to hold off unhappiness. The manic accumulation of things to off-set the gap between the world and your own expectations.

LANA: And what did I do with those things?

ELLEN: You gave them to me. Or rather, you left them with me. *[Sings]*
So sing me no songs of sorrow,
And tell me no tales of pain,
I keep a place within my heart
I call her Rosalaine.

LANA: So I came along just to leave these things and then go away again?

ELLEN: Sounds absurd, doesn't it?

LANA: It does. In fact, is seems hardly real at all. Did you give me anything?

ELLEN: Nothing you needed. Or at least nothing you wanted.

LANA: What do you think I needed?

ELLEN: I hardly know. It's so long ago and I was so wrong about the whole thing.

LANA: What did you do that was so wrong?

ELLEN: I just was. It was nothing I could really do anything about. At least not at the time. When you look back at yourself when you were younger, you see that you had time for everything except reflection, except change. I was just very busy about everything, almost manic in comparison with you. Ardent. You cast me in the role of some sort of uncouth emotional savage, totally oblivious of all reality, continuously committing emotional faux pas against those who knew the truth. In fact, you once gave me a copy of Proust (of course), do you remember? You wrote inside it: "To my dear Ellen – who waves all her leaves and flowers in the sun, who ardently refuses to wither into the truth." The thing is, for you the truth was outstandingly barren and hostile. I was always far more optimistic about life than you, which meant that around you I always felt like some sort of Sandra Dee figure. The really strange thing is that you envied me and resented what you thought was my ability to burn without burning up. That's what you really wanted from me — to see me burn up.

LANA: Did I hate you so much?

ELLEN: You didn't hate me. You just resented what I showed you – that there was something beyond your depression, but that you couldn't get at it.

End scene.

SCENE THREE:

A stage in the middle of a performance by GLENN, ELLEN and IMOGEN.

IMOGEN: *[Sings]*
The thing I like best is getting ready
There's quiet all over the set
There's nothing quite like anticipation
It's a wonderful feeling I get

The fans are in the shower
They won't be here for an hour.
I'm getting ready.

ELLEN: *[Sings]*
The thing I like best is getting ready
I love ord'ring house staff about.
I'm worried about tonight's takings
Last night half the house just walked out.

The punters are in a cab
Friday night is always drab.
I'm getting ready.

IMOGEN: *[Sings]*
The make-up, it smells like excitement
My costume still hums from last night
They loved it when I jumped that bloody wardrobe
The critics thought my gags out of sight

The audience are drinking gin
They are really shov'lling that stuff in
I'm getting ready.

IMOGEN AND ELLEN: *[Sing]*
The thing I like best is when it's over
The audience are happy and long gone
They're cashing in those theatre supper vouchers
They're catching their coaches to Geelong.

My lover's in the shower
I'll be with him in an hour
I'm getting ready.

End scene.

SCENE FOUR:

The theatre foyer is empty – it is after hours. IMOGEN is sitting by herself writing. LANA enters.

LANA: You're here late!

IMOGEN: So are you.

LANA: I can hardly keep away. The atmosphere is so compelling.

IMOGEN: Compelling is right. It's impossible to leave.

LANA: Is that really the way you feel?

IMOGEN: It is. I have been doing this stuff for about ten years. I'm not particularly good at it, at least I'm no better than a lot of others, and I can't seem to break away.

LANA: Do you feel like your mother is forcing you to stay?

IMOGEN: Not really. Perhaps. It's probably more to do with being scared of what's on the other side. It's all here for me, you see. I always wanted to do this and it used to make me happy. When we first started it was great. All the rehearsing and all the business of coming into the theatre and putting on the show, can you imagine how exciting that was for a nine-year-old?

LANA: I can.

IMOGEN: Now I feel like I'm in a rut. I'm frustrated and bored and I actually feel a little bit guilty that I'm not enjoying myself more. Most of the people who come to see us would probably kill for the chance to do all this. I think I take it out on Ellen, but it's not really her fault. She doesn't help, of course, but, the thing is, she doesn't really understand me. Is that too much of a cliché?

LANA: It is but the fact that we all go through it at some time tends to suggest that it's true.

IMOGEN: Did you go through it with your mother?

LANA: Not exactly, but it doesn't have to be your mother. You will probably find that there are hundreds of people out there who seem to be hanging around waiting to patronise you. It's not a maternal monopoly, but it is a fairly parental instinct.

IMOGEN: I don't think I have ever really thought of Ellen as parental. She's far more producer than parent. If she were just an annoying mother I don't think I would mind as much.

LANA: I have to admit, she's not exactly the maternal type.

IMOGEN: Sometimes I think she only had us so that we could play the kids' parts in *Hay Fever*. God, all that whinging about people who have

	kids to provide the body parts for their other kids. I want a UN charter on the rights of the unborn theatrical child.
LANA:	I imagine it's a fairly complicated relationship.
IMOGEN:	Complicated? It's like being mothered by Margaret Thatcher.
LANA:	I knew a woman once that was a lot like your mother.
IMOGEN:	What was she like?
LANA:	Beautiful.
IMOGEN:	Great, just what everyone thinks about Ellen.
LANA:	I was probably fairly biased.
IMOGEN:	Why?
LANA:	Well, you know.
IMOGEN:	Did you have the hots for her?
LANA:	To put it mildly.
IMOGEN:	My God, are you gay?
LANA:	Of course.
IMOGEN:	I'm so stupid. I never realised.
LANA:	No you're not. We just never really had a sex talk.

IMOGEN: God, how boring we must be? Hey, you're not in love with me are you?

LANA: No. I'm just in love with the idea of you.

IMOGEN: You are then! That's the only way any boy has ever been in love with me. Anyway, tell me the details. Who was she?

LANA: It was a long time ago. You wouldn't know her. We were working together, or at least that's how we met. She had a husband and a couple of kids, so it was all a bit out of the blue for her. She had not been working for years and on her first job she was landed with me. It was incredibly intense and romantic, lots of long walks and long lunches, but not much in the physical sense.

IMOGEN: Why not?

LANA: I think it was all a bit of an experiment for her. She seemed very ambitious. She had had a number of years outside the workforce and when she finally made it back I think she found it all very exciting and, obviously, she wanted to get on.

IMOGEN: What, you mean she was using you?

LANA: Not really. At least I don't think it was a conscious thing for her. I just think some people have a tendency to confuse the difference between love and work. Love and work are the only things really worth doing, you see, so it's easy to fall into the trap of conflating them. That's probably your mother's problem.

IMOGEN: So what happened?

LANA: We were inseparable for a few months while we were working together and then for a little bit afterwards. As a real relationship though, it didn't really seem to be going anywhere. She became involved somehow with a guy we were working with and about that time I moved on. A protective move I think.

IMOGEN: What, she started sleeping with him?

LANA: Probably not – just lots of long walks and long lunches.

IMOGEN: Did you ever see her again?

LANA: No. I gather she has become quite successful, though.

IMOGEN: Whoever said the working lunch was over?

LANA: Indeed. And being side-by-side on the treadmill at the gym was never going to be as sexy as a walk in the park

IMOGEN: Do you think about her much?

LANA: Sometimes.

End scene.

SCENE FIVE:

The theatre foyer is empty – it is after hours. ELLEN is messing about with box office things and GLENN comes in as if off for the night.

GLENN: Has everyone gone?

ELLEN: It didn't take them long. *[She holds up the receipts]* Hardly a huge house.

GLENN: That's a pity. I was looking forward to talking to that cute girl in the fourth row.

ELLEN: I didn't really think she was your type. Let alone your age. Anyway she left at interval. Didn't you notice?

GLENN: You wrote the play – I'm hardly on in the second half. Look, we have to sort this thing about between you and Imogen, it's killing the show.

ELLEN: My Oedipal drama is hardly any problem for the punters. In fact we should leak it to *Who Weekly*. I would be great for business.

GLENN: Oedipus! You've obviously been having one of your little sessions with Lana.

ELLEN: You're just the tiniest little bit disturbed by all that. Aren't you?

GLENN: I don't do anything in tiny bits. I am madly jealous and green with envy.

ELLEN: I think you are. Or at least you don't understand that kind of relationship – or you understand it very well and you are jealous of it.

GLENN: We should save this for the show.

ELLEN: Bloody hell, Glenn. This is really pissing me off. I know it's stupid and absurd, but ten years ago something happened to me. I met someone who changed my life. I know that sounds idiotic and naïve to you – who seem to be able to walk through life avoiding the emotional fringe – but to me, at that time of my life that friendship meant something to me. Just as your friendship means something to me now. Who knows, probably as a result of this weekend, I'll be telling someone a story about you in ten years. The point is, Lana walked in and out on me and I never found out why. I am over her, but I am not over wondering why. If you can tell me what it is about me that makes me so repellent to people I like – as you obviously know – then I would be much obliged.

GLENN: If you think that's going to make me hold back on telling you about your problems with Imogen, you are wrong.

ELLEN: *[About to walk]* Go to hell.

Act 1 - Scene 5

GLENN: No, look, I'm sorry. You are right – I'm being totally insensitive. This Lana thing is just irritating me. I suppose I am a little jealous. I mean, we have a past too. Don't get me wrong, if you came near me again I would certainly throw up – but no one likes to see their place in history downgraded. It irritates me to see you getting sucked in by that totally neurotic woman.

ELLEN: Would you rather I got sucked in by you?

GLENN: Of course.

ELLEN: You dumped me, I seem to remember.

GLENN: You like that, don't you! It helps you assemble you little emotional schemes in the comfort and convenience of your own home.

ELLEN: I am not a schemer. I just like situations.

GLENN: So what is her excuse anyway?

ELLEN: Excuse?

GLENN: Why did she walk out on you?

ELLEN: I don't know. I haven't found out.

GLENN: What did she say? You did ask her!

ELLEN: We had better not discuss this.

GLENN: Tell me you asked her.

ELLEN: Look, Glenn, let's drop it.

GLENN:	You are pathetic.
ELLEN:	That is exactly why I don't want to talk about it. You're so bloody insensitive...
GLENN:	OK, I'm sorry, I'll shut up. Just tell me what happened.
ELLEN:	I kind of asked her. But she just doesn't give anything back.
GLENN:	Did you just ask her straight out?
ELLEN:	Sort of.
GLENN:	This is too weird.
ELLEN:	Well I did. It's just that she deflects everything so well.
GLENN:	What, you mean she's avoiding the issue?
ELLEN:	Kind of. But it's more like she's gone into this ultra-analyst persona, deflecting everything back as if nothing has really touched her.
GLENN:	It sounds like she has totally closed down.
ELLEN:	Maybe. But I kind of half suspect that she's taking on some sort of transference identity. I mean, she talks in the first person—"what did I do then?", "Why did I hate you?". At first I thought she might have forgotten it all – or rather, repressed it in one of her breakdowns. But then I got the impression that she was just humouring me. Playing some sort of analyst

Act 1 - Scene 5

          game in which she became the Lana I wanted her to be. A complete and pure projection of my ego.

GLENN: God. This sounds like, *Hiroshima Mon Amour*.

ELLEN: Exactly!

GLENN: That wasn't meant to be a good thing. So, why didn't you just break it up and get her to be straight with you?

ELLEN: I don't know. You have to understand, it was a pretty charged situation. I wasn't exactly in full possession of my emotions. Besides, she's a mesmerising character – very emotionally manipulative.

GLENN: So what are you going to do about it?

ELLEN: I don't know. You are better at the direct approach that I am. What do you suggest?

GLENN: Next time you speak to her you should just make her deal with it all. Go in there with a singleness of purpose and get some answers. Threaten to walk if she doesn't fess up.

ELLEN: What happens if she walks?

GLENN: I don't think she will. She's gone to a bit of trouble to get this far – she definitely wants something. Make her work for it.

ELLEN: It's a big risk, for me.

GLENN: Rubbish. What are you afraid of?

End scene.

Scene Six:

The theatre foyer is empty – it is after hours. LANA is singing and GLENN and ELLEN are playing guitar and cello just off stage.

LANA: *[Sings]*
Take oh take my soul for it's eternal
Cover it in merriment and mirth.
Watch it fondly when it flies to Heaven
Gather it gently when it falls to Earth

Come to me darling and sit very near,
My eyes are now wide open and my mind's becoming clear.

Bend, not break my heart now that you hold it
Feel it beat as if your very own.
I once gave you naught but my true love, dear
Now you leave me empty here alone.

Think of me sometimes, and my love indeed.
Don't ask me for anything – you have everything you need.

End scene.

SCENE SEVEN:

The theatre foyer is empty – it is after hours. ELLEN and LANA are sitting and talking.

ELLEN: Do you mind if I ask what you want with my daughter?

LANA: What I want with your daughter?

ELLEN: Where did you track her down?

LANA: I didn't track her down. We met at uni when I went back to do psych.

ELLEN: Does she know about you and me?

LANA: About you and me? What do you mean "about you and me"?

ELLEN: About our relationship?

LANA: What was our relationship?

ELLEN: Don't you know?

LANA: I'm interested in what you know.

ELLEN: I don't know anything. All I know is that one minute you and I were inseparable, really close. The next minute you were gone. Then

	ten years later you walk in here arm-in-arm with my daughter. I don't understand any of it. Obviously, I am totally clueless.
LANA:	I have never talked to her about you at all.
ELLEN:	Oh.
LANA:	I have decided I am not going to see you. If you still want to see someone, I'll find you someone else.
ELLEN:	That's probably a good idea.
LANA:	You're happy with that?
ELLEN:	I don't know, but it's probably for the best.
LANA:	You are angry with me for coming here this weekend.
ELLEN:	No I am not.
LANA:	You are very defensive.
ELLEN:	No I am not. I don't even really know what that means.
LANA:	So you don't mind if I suggest you see someone else?
ELLEN:	Not at all.
LANA:	Thank you. It's very understanding of you. I would stay on but you seem to think there is nothing I can give you and I suspect you're right.

Act I - Scene 7

ELLEN: We've been here before.

LANA: Apparently. I'm sorry. Goodbye.

ELLEN: Bye.

LANA starts moving off.

ELLEN: Lana! I have to ask you.

LANA: What?

ELLEN: What happened with us?

LANA: Do you think this will make you feel any better? Let's just imagine that I could give you any kind of response you might want. In a minute from now you might think you had some sort of closure. But in a day you will just be feeling the same way again.

ELLEN: So why not just give me some temporary relief?

LANA: Because it's not about me. It's not even about Imogen.

ELLEN: Surely not.

LANA: Ellen, I didn't abandon you. You cut me off. You had this totally mundane view of how I was going to fit into your world. You left me because you don't know how to be with someone unless you own them. Or unless they own you.

ELLEN: What so I cut you off because I decided I wasn't gay?

LANA: No. You didn't cut me off because I was a woman. You cut me off because you thought I was sad. What you wanted from me was melancholy – my socially acceptable sadness. Anything beyond that was too much for you.

ELLEN: That's unfair.

LANA: No it's not. Your problem with me was the same problem you have with Imogen. You are the maker of melancholy, and no one else is allowed any of it. Or rather, you only want others to be sad to the point where you still get to set the levels. Do you ever read any of your own plays? If you did you would know that anyone in your life who shows any real sense of loss threatens you. Sadness is a plaything to you, but the sight of real loss makes you afraid of losing control all together. You envied me only up to the point before I went over the edge. Then you climbed back, to your husband, then even to Glenn, totally afraid that I would pull you down with me. You feel the danger even more keenly with Imogen, of course. She's not allowed any real sadness because you are afraid you will totally dissolve in her grief. When she goes off, you know you will go with her – over the edge completely. That is why you cut me off. Ellen, meine liebe, I was the forerunner.

ELLEN: But you just left me there. We weren't a case study. We were friends. Don't you have any sense of remorse?

LANA: But you're still blaming me. How can I take you seriously? You still can't work out if it's my story or yours. In fact, you don't even know whether it really happened.

Curtain.

www.ingramcontent.com/pod-product-compliance
Lightning Source LLC
Chambersburg PA
CBHW071321080526
44587CB00018B/3306